D.F. Lemmon

**The Ancient Capital of the State of Indiana, Corydon,**

**Harrison County**

D.F. Lemmon

**The Ancient Capital of the State of Indiana, Corydon, Harrison County**

ISBN/EAN: 9783337149475

Printed in Europe, USA, Canada, Australia, Japan

Cover: Foto ©Suzi / pixelio.de

More available books at **www.hansebooks.com**

# THE

## ANCIENT CAPITAL

### OF THE

# STATE OF INDIANA,

# CORYDON,

## HARRISON COUNTY,

### BY

## D. F. LEMMON.

# PREFACE.

In publishing this work it has been my object to give to the public interesting information in regard to the beginning and formation of one of the greatest States in the Union, Indiana. Corydon was established as the seat of our Territorial government in 1813, while we were in the midst of our second war with Great Britain. From Corydon went up the petition to Congress from our territorial fathers, asking to be admitted into the Union of States, and to have Indiana added to the great galaxy as a free and independent State, on the same footing with original States. It was to the old pioneer fathers at Corydon that Congress promptly replied, granting their petition. It was at Corydon that the first Constitution of the State was formed and adopted. It was at Corydon that the first laws for the government of the people of the State were made. It was at the time-honored town of Corydon that the State of Indiana was born, nourished and fondled in infancy, reared and trained in youth, that gave her the impetus to mature into giantry.

During all this time here clustered the heroic and patriotic pioneers, and giant intellects of the State. Forgetfulness is very near unto all. In the boundless, wondrous jostle of things, our lives and our deaths are lost sight of. The panorama is shifted, and the life-bustle of to-day is the death-tableau of to-morrow. And while it is extremely difficult to recover from the dim and shadowy past, a true history of all the struggles and privations of the pioneers—of their hardships, trials and sufferings; of their victories, experiences of hope and faith; of their disappointments and triumphs, still we have their places of action, as well as many of their acts, together with their historic and sacred names, which we present in these pages and which, we doubt not, will be appreciated and greatly cherished by the noble sons and daughters of the great State of Indiana

Being engaged in writing a full and complete history of Harrison, the old Capitol County, I have selected the matter contained herein for the benefit and edification of the people throughout our State.

The Author,

D. F. LEMMON.

Corydon, Indiana, October, 1891.

# THE ANCIENT CAPITAL.

Harrison County, within the boundaries of which is the time-honored town, and first State Capital of Indiana, Corydon, was named in honor of the first Territorial Governor of Indiana, William Henry Harrison, the distinguished patriot, soldier and statesman. It was the fourth county organized—carved from a portion of the territory included in Knox county, in 1808, and is situated in the southern portion of the State. It is bounded north by Washington county, east by Floyd county, south-east, south, and south-west by the Ohio river, which runs on its border about sixty miles, west by Crawford county, and contains 478 square miles, and a population of 22,000. The settlement of this county, by the whites, dates back to the beginning of the present century. In common with the entire southern part of the State, it is somewhat broken and hilly, but possesses some beautiful and fertile valleys. The uplands have no superiors in the State for small grains and fruit, which are produced in abundance. The wheat yield this year being estimated at fully one million bushels. There are many attractive caves, and beautiful streams of water within its limits. The population of this county being principally descendants from the old sturdy pioneers, who came here nearly a century ago, and the balance being excellent people from the older States, they are intelligent, civil, industrious, economical and progressive. Indeed no other county in our State, has better society than the "old Capitol County."

While there are not many wealthy people in our county, it has often and truthfully been said, by persons who travel extensively, that in proportion to population, no other county in the State had more good livers than this county, and the generosity and hospitality of whose people knew no bounds: and as the old pioneer fathers, whose characteristics they have inherited, the latch-string always hangs outward.

The Ancient Capital, Corydon, the seat of justice, and the geographical and legal center of the county, was founded in 1808, by William Henry Harrison and Hervey Heth. It is a beautiful town, pleasantly situated in a valley, and on the high rolling ground at the junction of Big and Little Indian creeks. It is surrounded on all sides by high hills, from which grand views of the surrounding country may be obtained. It is 120 miles due south of Indianapolis, 20 miles west of the Falls Cities, New Albany, Jeffersonville and Louisville, and 8 miles east of the noted Wyandotte Cave, 7 miles south of the L., E. & St. L. Railroad, by which it is connected by the Louisville, New Albany & Corydon Railroad.

At the suggestion of Gov. Harrison, this town was named by Miss Jennie Smith, daughter of Edward Smith, a deserter from the British army, during the Revolutionary War. Some years after Mr. Smith deserted he worked his way into the wilderness where Corydon now stands. A few rods east of the Fair Ground spring, just south of the present corporate limits of Corydon, Mr. Smith erected a log cabin, where he reared a large, intelligent and respectable family. While Gen. Harrison was Govenor of Indiana Territory, at Vincennes, he made frequent visits east, and also spent a part of his time in Harrison county, and while on those visits, he always made Mr. Smith's cabin one of his stopping points, where he rested his wearied limbs, and his jaded "nag."

The General was very fond of vocal music, and Mr. Smith's daughters were good singers. They had procured a song book in which was the song "Old Corydon." This was the General's favorite, and he, on his visits, had the young ladies sing it, and frequently to repeat it; and often after supper the General and the Smith family would gather in front of the cabin door while those noble young pioneer heroines would make the hills and valleys, around where Corydon now stands, resound with their musical strains, perhaps drowning the screams of the wiley and sneaking panther, and the howls of the impudent and daring wolves. On taking his leave of the family, one morning, the General suggested to the young ladies that he intended to found a town near by, and requested a name, whereupon Miss

Jennie Smith suggested that it be called after his favorite song, *Corydon*, which was accepted by the General.

By an act of the General Assembly of Indiana Territory, at Vincennes, which was approved on the 11th day of March, 1813, the Seat of Government of said Territory was fixed at Corydon, Harrison County, "from and after the first day of May, 1813."

In conformity with a joint resolution of both Houses of the General Assembly of the Territory, Acting Governor Gibson prorogued them to meet at Corydon on the first day of December, 1813. Corydon remained the Territorial and State Capital of Indiana, from that date until the tenth day of January, 1825, when it was removed to Indianapolis. The population of this ancient town is near one thousand, which is not much greater than it was while it was the Capital of the State.

While Corydon is not large it is quite a business place. And as it is in the natural gas area, many fine natural gas wells being near by, her enterprising citizens hope, in the near future, to see her greatly stimulated by the same.

THE OLD STATE CAPITAL AT CORYDON, 1813–25.

This old stone structure was built in 1811, but not thoroughly completed until 1815. Dennis Pennington, one of the most prominent men in Harrison county, and in fact in the State, in his time, superintended the building of it. It is forty feet square. The foundation was placed three feet in the ground and made two and one-half feet wide. The walls for the first story are two and one half feet thick, and the room fifteen feet high in the clear. The walls of the second story are two feet thick and the room ten feet in the clear. The material out of which this building was constructed was blue lime-stone, in irregular courses, from four to twelve inches thick, gathered from the immediate neighborhood. The Legislature met here until 1825. The members of the House occupied the lower room, and the Senate Chamber was the room in the south side of the upper story. The Clerk of the Supreme Court occupied a room in the north-east corner of the second story. When the Legislature was not in session these rooms were occupied by the Supreme, District, and County Courts.

This old building has been used extensively for the last eighty years. United States Senators have been elected here. Presidential Electors have been elected here, and cast their votes for Presidential candidates here. It has been used since

THE OLD STATE CAPITAL AT CORYDON, 1813–25.

it has been built for all parties in holding their political conventions here. It is the grand center for all kinds of public gatherings. And although used so extensively for the last four score years, not a single break appears in its massive walls. It has for several years been used as the Circuit Court building.

The Court occupying the lower floor, and the juries the rooms of the upper story.

The General Assembly of Indiana Territory, which met at Corydon on the first Monday in December, 1815, did on the 14th day of that month, adopt a memorial which was laid before Congress, by the Territorial Delegate, the Hon. Jonathan Jennings, on the 28th of the same month, that contained the following passages: "Whereas, the Ordinance of Congress for the government of this Territory has provided, that when there shall be sixty thousand free inhabitants therein, this Territory shall be admitted into the Union on an equal footing with the original States; and, whereas, by a census taken by the authority of the Legislature of this Territory, it appears from the returns, that the number of free white inhabitants, exceeds sixty thousand—We, therefore, pray the Honorable Senate and House of Representatives, in Congress assembled, to order an election, to be conducted agreeably to the existing laws of this Territory to be held in the several counties of this Territory, *on the first Monday of May*, 1816, for Representatives to meet in Convention, at the seat of Government of this Territory, on the —— day of ——, 1816, who, when assembled, shall determine, by a majority of the votes of all the members elected, whether it will be expedient or inexpedient to go into a State Government; and if it be determined expedient, the Convention thus assembled shall have the power to form a Constitution and frame of Government; or, if it be deemed inexpedient, to provide for the election of Representatives to meet in Convention, at some future period, to form a Constitution.

"And, whereas, the inhabitants of this Territory are principally composed of emigrants from every part of the Union, and as various in their customs and sentiments as in their persons, we think it prudent, at this time, to express to the General Government our attachment to the fundamental principles of legislation prescribed by Congress in their ordinance for the government of this Territory, particularly, as respects *personal freedom* and *involuntary servitude*, and hope they may be continued as the basis of the Constitution."

The Memorial was referred to a committee, of which Mr.

Jennings, the Delegate from Indiana Territory, was the chairman; and on the 5th of January, 1816, this gentleman reported to the House of Representatives of the United States, a bill to enable the people of the Indiana Territory to form a Constitution and State Government, and for the admission of such State into the Union on an equal footing with the original States. This bill, after having been amended in some particulars, was passed by Congress, and became a law, by the approval of the President of the United States, on the 19th day of April, 1816. Which act is as follows:

ACT OF CONGRESS.

**An Act to enable the people of the Indiana Territory to form a Constitution and State Government, and for the admission of such State into the Union on equal footing with the original States.**

(Approved April 16, 1815.)

Section 1. Be it enacted by the Senate and the House of Representatives, of the United States of America, in Congress assembled:

That the inhabitants of the Territory of Indiana be, and they are hereby authorized, to form for themselves a Constitution and State Government, and to assume such name as they shall deem proper; and the said State when formed, shall be admitted into the Union upon the same footing with the original States, in all respects whatever.

Sec. 2. And be it further enacted, that the said State shall consist of all the territory included within the following boundaries, to-wit: Bounded on the East by the meridian line which forms the western boundry of the State of Ohio; on the South, by the river Ohio, from the mouth of the Great Miami river to the mouth of the river Wabash; on the West, by a line drawn from the middle of the Wabash, from its mouth to a point where a due north line drawn from the town of Vincennes would last touch the north-western shore of the said river; and from thence, by a due north line, until the same shall intersect an east and west line drawn through a point ten miles north of the southern extreme of Lake Michigan; on the North by the said east and west line, until the same shall intersect the first mentioned meridian line, which forms the western boundry of the State of Ohio; provided that the convention hereinafter provided for, when formed, shall ratify the boundaries aforesaid; otherwise they shall be and remain as now prescribed by the ordinance for the government of the Territory north-west of the river Ohio; provided, also, that the said State shall have concurrent jurisdiction on the river Wabash, with the State to be formed west thereof, so far as the said river shall form a common boundary to both.

Sec. 3. AND BE IT FURTHER ENACTED, That all male citizens of the United States, who shall have arrived at the age of twenty-one years, and resided within the said Territory at least one year previous to the day of election, and shall have paid a county or territorial tax, and all persons having in other respects the legal qualifications to vote for Representatives in the General Assembly by the said Territory, be, and they are hereby authorized to choose Representatives to form a Convention, who shall be apportioned among the several counties within the said Territory, according to the apportionment made by the Legislature thereof, at their last session, to-wit: From the county of Wayne, four representatives; from the county of Dearborn, three representatives; from the county of Switzerland, one representative; from the county of Jefferson, three representatives; from the county of Clark, five representatives; from the county of Harrison, five representatives; from the county of Washington, five representatives; from the county of Knox, five representatives; from the county of Gibson, four representatives; from the county of Posey, one representative; from the county of Warrick, one representative; from the county of Perry, one representative.

And the election for the representatives aforesaid, shall be holden on the second Monday in May, One thousand eight hundred and sixteen, throughout the several counties in said Territory; and shall be conducted in the same manner, and under the same penalties as prescribed by the laws of said Territory regulating elections therein for members of the House of Representatives.

Sec. 4. And be it further enacted, that the members of the Convention, thus duly elected, be, and they are hereby authorized, to meet at the seat of government of said Territory, on

the second Monday of June next. which Convention when met,
shall first determine, by a majority of the whole number elected, whether it be or be not expedient, at that time, to form a
Constitution and State Government for the people within the
said Territory: and if it be determined to be expedient, the
Convention shall be, and hereby are, authorized to form a Constitution and State Government; or if it be deemed more expedient, the said Convention shall provide by Ordinance for election of representatives to form a Constitution or frame of government, which said representatives shall be chosen in such
manner, and in such proportion, and shall meet at such time
and place, as shall be prescribed by the said Ordinance; and
shall then form, for the people of said Territory, a Constitution
and State Government; provided, that the same, whenever
formed, shall be republican, and not repugnant to those articles of the Ordinance of the thirteenth of July, One thousand
seven hundred and eighty-seven, which are declared to be irrevocable between the original States and the people and States
of the territory north-west of the river Ohio; excepting so much
of said articles as relates to the boundaries of States therein to
be formed.

SEC. 5.   AND BE IT FURTHER ENACTED, That until the next
general census shall be taken, the said State shall be entitled
to one Representative in the House of Representatives of the
United States.

SEC. 6.   AND BE IT FURTHER ENACTED, That the following
propositions be, and the same are hereby offered to the Convention of the said Territory of Indiana, when formed, for their
free acceptance or rejection, which, if accepted by the Convention shall be obligatory upon the United States:

*First.* That the section numbered sixteen, in every township,
and when such section has been sold, granted, or disposed of,
other lands, equivalant thereto, and most contiguous to the
same, shall be granted to the inhabitants of such township, for
the use of schools.

*Second.* That all salt springs within the said Territory, and
the land reserved for the use of the same, together with such
other lands as may, by the President of the United States, be
deemed necessary and proper for working the said salt springs,
not exceeding in the whole, the quantity contained in thirty-

six entire sections, shall be granted to the said State for use of
the people of the said State, the same to be used under such
terms, conditions, and regulations as the Legislature of the
said State shall direct; provided, the said Legislature shall nev-
er sell nor lease the same for a longer period than ten years at
any one time.

*Third.* That five per cent. of the net proceeds of the lands
lying within the said Territory, and which shall be sold by
Congress, from and after the first day of December next, after
deducting all expenses incident to the same, shall be reserved
for making public roads and canals, of which three-fifths shall be
applied to those objects within the said State, under the direction
of the Legislature thereof, and two-fifths to the making of a
road or roads leading to the said State under the direction of
Congress.

*Fourth.* That one entire township, which shall be designated
by the President of the United States, in addition to the one
heretofore reserved for the use of a seminary of learning, and
vested in the Legislature of the said State, to be appropriated
solely to the use of such seminary by the said Legislature.

*Fifth.* That four sections of land be, and the same are hereby granted to the said State, for the purpose of fixing their
seat of Government thereon, which four sections shall, under
the direction of the Legislature of said State, be located at any
time in such township and range, as the Legislature, aforesaid,
may select, on such lands as may hereafter be acquired by the
United States, from the Indian tribes within said Territory;
provided that such locations shall be made prior to the public
sale of the lands of the United States, surrounding such loca-
tion; and, *provided always*, that the five foregoing propositions
herein offered, are on the conditions: that the Convention of the
said State shall provide by an ordinance irrevocable, without
the consent of the United States, that every and each tract of
land sold by the United States, from and after the first day of
December next, shall be and remain exempt from any tax, laid
by order or under any authority of the State, whether for State,
county, or township, or for any other purpose whatever, for the
term of five years, from and after the day of sale."

In conformity with the provisions of this law, an election for
members of a Convention, to form a State Constitution, was

held in the several counties of the Territory, on Monday, the
thirteenth day of May, 1816. The members of the Convention
were elected according to an apportionment which had been
made by the Territorial Legislature, and confirmed by an act
of Congress. Their names and the names of the counties which
they represented in the Convention, here follow:

CLARK COUNTY, five members, Jonathan Jennings, James
Scott, Thomas Carr, John K. Graham, and James Lemmon.

KNOX COUNTY. five members. John Johnson, John Badollet,
William Polke, Benjamin Parke, and John Benefiel.

DEARBORN COUNTY, three members, James Dill, Solomon
Manwaring, and Ezra Ferris.

HARRISON COUNTY, five members, Dennis Pennington, Davis
Floyd, Daniel C. Lane, John Boone, and Patrick Shields.

WAYNE COUNTY, four members, Jeremiah Cox, Patrick Baird, Joseph Holman, and Hugh Cull.

FRANKLIN COUNTY, five members, William H. Eads, James
Brownlee, Enoch McCarty, Robert Hanna, jr., and James Noble.

SWITZERLAND COUNTY, one member, William Cotton.

JEFFERSON COUNTY, three members, David H. Maxwell,
Samuel Smock, and Nathaniel Hunt.

WASHINGTON COUNTY, five members, John DePauw, Samuel
Milroy, Robert McIntyre, William Lowe, and William Graham.

GIBSON COUNTY, four members, David Robb, James Smith,
Alexander Devin, and Frederick Rapp.

WARRICK COUNTY, one member. Daniel Grass.

PERRY COUNTY, one member, Charles Polke.

POSEY COUNTY, one member, Dann Lynn.

The Convention commenced its session, at Corydon, on the
10th of June, 1816, and continued to meet from day to day,
until the 29th of June; when, having completed the work of
forming a State Constitution, the members closed the session
by final adjournment.

Hon. Jonathan Jennings was President, and Hon. William
Hendricks was Secretary, of the Convention; and both were future Governors of the State.

On the 3rd day of the Convention the President, Mr. Jennings, announced the appointment of the following Committees:

Committee to prepare a Bill of Rights and Preamble to the Constitution, Messrs. Badollet, Manwaring, Graham, of Clark, Lane, Smith, and Pennington.

Committee relative to the distribution of the Powers of Government, Messrs. Johnson, Polke, of Perry, Floyd, Maxwell and McCarty.

Committee relative to the Legislative Department of Government, Messrs. Noble, Ferris, Milroy, Benefiel, and Grass.

Committee relative to the Executive Department of Government, Messrs. Graham, of Clark, Polke, of Knox, Rappe, Shields, Smock, Smith, Ferris, and Brownlee.

Committee relative to the Judicial Department of Government, Messrs. Scott, Johnson, Dill, Milroy, Noble, Cotton, Lowe, Park, and Hunt.

Committee relative to Impeachments, Messrs. Dill, Cox, Hunt, Eads, and Carr.

Committee relative to general provisions for the Constitution not embraced in the subjects refered to other Committees, Messrs. Maxwell, DePauw, Robb. Scott. and Baird.

Committee relative to the mode of revising the Constitution. Messrs. Hanna, Pennington. Devin, Johnson, and Graham, of Washington.

Committee relative to the change of Government and preserving the existing laws until repealed by the State Legislature, and providing for appeals from the Territorial Courts to the State Courts, Messrs. Floyd, Lemmon, Holman. McIntyre, Manwaring, and Benefiel.

Committee relative to education and the universal dissemination of useful knowledge, and other objects which it might be deemed proper to enjoin or advise the State Legislature to provide for, Messrs. Scott, Badollet, Polke, of Knox, Lynn, and Boone.

Committee relative to the Militia, Messrs. Dill, Hanna, Carr, Cotton, Robb, Holman, Cox, DePauw, Noble, Rappe, and Benefiel.

Committee relative to Elective Franchise and Elections, Messrs. Ferris, Lemmon, Grass, Polke, of Perry, Cull, Smith, and DePauw.

Committee on Prisons, Messrs. Carr, Pennington, Milroy, Grass, Hunt, Graham, of Washington, and McCarty.

## ORDINANCE ADOPTED.

"Be it Ordained by the Representatives of the People of
the Territory of Indiana, in Convention met at Corydon, on Monday, the tenth day of June, in the year of
our Lord, Eighteen hundred and sixteen,

That we do, for ourselves and our posterity, agree, determine,
declare, and ordain, that we will, and do hereby, accept the
propositions of the Congress of the United States, as made
and contained in their act of the nineteenth day of April, Eighteen hundred and sixteen, entitled, "An act to enable the people of the Indiana Territory to form a State Government and
Constitution, and for the admission of such State into the Union,
on an equal footing with the original States."

And we do, further, for ourselves and our posterity, hereby
ratify, confirm, and establish, the boundaries of the said State
of Indiana, as fixed, prescribed, laid down, and established, in
the act of Congress aforesaid, and we do also, further, for ourselves, and our posterity, hereby agree, determine, declare, and
ordain, that each and every tract of land sold by the United
States, lying within the said State, and which shall be sold
from and after the first day of December next, shall be and
remain exempt from any tax laid by order, or under any authority of the said State of Indiana, or by or under the authority
of the General Assembly thereof, whether for State, county, or
township, or any other purpose whatever, for the term of five
years from and after the day of sale of any such tract of land;
and we do, moreover, for ourselves and our posterity, hereby
declare and ordain this Ordinance, and every part thereof,
shall forever be and remain irrevocable and inviolate, without
the consent of the United States, in Congress assembled, first
had and obtained for the alteration thereof, or any part thereof.

JONATHAN JENNINGS,
President of the Convention.

Attest: WILLIAM HENDRICKS, Secretary.
June 29, 1816."

---

## PREAMBLE TO THE CONSTITUTION.

We, the Representatives of the people of the Territory of

Indiana, in Convention, met at Corydon, on Monday, the tenth day of June, in the year of our Lord, Eighteen hundred and sixteen, and of the Independence of the United States the fortieth, having the right of admission into the General Government, as a member of the Union, consistent with the Constitution of the United States, the Ordinance of Congress of One thousand seven hundred and eighty-seven, and the Law of Congress entitled, "An Act to enable the people of Indiana Territory to form a Constitution and State Government, and for the admission of such State into the Union on an equal footing with the original States," in order to establish justice, promote the welfare, and secure the blessings of liberty to ourselves and our posterity, do ordain, and establish the following Constitution or form of Government; and do mutually agree, with each other, to form ourselves into a free and independent State, by the name of *The State of Indiana.*

THE CONSTITUTIONAL TREE.

When the old hardy pioneer Delegates met at Corydon on the 10th of June, 1816, to draft our first Constitution, and to formulate plans of government, for a future great State of the

Union, Indiana, the most of them had left their abodes, rude log cabins, and had traveled many miles through an almost unbroken wilderness, infested with the wild cat, the catamount, the panther, the bear, the wolf, &c.

They had chased the deer, and had contended with the savages of the forests, the Indians, and were used to out-door exercise; and rather than be seated in a large, commodious, and cosey room of the "*Ancient Capital*" building, during their entire session, in the hot days of June, from the 10th, to the 29th, they hied themselves to the inviting shades of the spreading boughs of a huge Elm, on the banks of Big Indian creek, about two squares north-west of the Capital building, where they spent about half their time, of their twenty days, devising ways and means to secure to their posterity, and the future generations, a happy and prosperous people, a wise and good government.

The old Elm still stands in all of its grandure; one hundred and twenty-four feet from tip to tip of its branches, five feet in diameter, and about fifty feet high. It was photographed in the spring of 1891, for this work, and the foregoing is an exact picture of it. This mammoth Elm is sacredly cherished by all the inhabitants of the "Ancient Capital." and greatly admired by all who behold it. Long may it wave.

———

The Convention that formed the first Constitution of the State of Indiana, was composed mainly of clear minded, unpretending men, of common sense and rugged honesty, who were aglow with patriotism, and whose morals were not questioned. Seeing and feeling their need of good government, they had familiarized themselves with the imperishable principles and theories of that grand instrument, the Declaration of Independence, handed down by the fathers of 1776. The Constitution of the United States was also investigated and cherished by them as a sacred message. The Constitution that was formed for Indiana, in 1816, was clear and concise, comprehensive and just, for the maintenance of civil and religious liberty, designed to protect the rights of the people, and to provide for the public welfare.

The officers of the Territorial Government were required to

# 19

continue to discharge their duties until superseded by officers elected under the Constitution of the State. The President of the Convention was required to "issue writs of election, directed to the several Sheriffs of the several counties requiring them to cause an election to be held for Governor, Lieutenant-Governor, Representative to Congress, members of the General Assembly, Sheriffs, and Coroners, at their respective election districts, in each county, on the first Monday in August, 1816." At the general election which was held at this time, Hon. Jonathan Jennings, of Clark county, was elected Governor. He received 5,211 votes; and his competitor, Gov. Thomas Posey, of Harrison county, who was the Governor of the Territory, received 3,934 votes. Christopher Harrison, of Washington county, was elected Lieutenant-Governor; and William Hendricks, of Jefferson county, was elected Representative to Congress.

The election of members of the first General Assembly, under the Constitution of the State of Indiana, resulted as follows:

SENATE.

From the county of Knox, William Polke.
From the county of Gibson, William Prince.
From the counties of Posey, Perry, and Warrick, Daniel Grass.
From the county of Wayne, Patrick Baird.
From the county of Franklin, John Conner.
From the counties of Washington, Orange, and Jackson, John DePauw.
From the counties of Jefferson and Switzerland, John Paul.
From the county of Dearborn, Ezra Ferris.
From the county of Harrison, Dennis Pennington.
From the county of Clark, James Beggs.

HOUSE.

From the county of Wayne, Joseph Holman, Ephraim Overman, and John Scott.
From the county of Franklin, James Noble, David Mounts, and James Brownlee.

From the county of Dearborn, Amos Lane, and Erasmus Powell.

From the county of Switzerland, John Dumont.

From the county of Jefferson, Williamson Dunn and Samuel Alexander.

From the county of Clark, Benjamin Ferguson, Thomss Carr, and John K. Graham.

From the county of Harrison, Davis Floyd, Jacob Zenor, and John Boone.

From the county of Washington, Samuel Milroy and Alexander Littell.

From the county of Jackson, William Graham.

From the county of Orange, Jonathan Lindley.

From the county of Knox, Isaac Blackford, Walter Wilson, and Henry I. Mills.

From the county of Gibson, Edmond Hogan and John Johnson.

From the county of Posey, Dann Lynn.

From the county of Warrick, Ratliff Boone.

From the county of Perry, Samuel Conner.

The Assembly commenced its session, at Corydon, on Monday, the 4th of November, 1816.

John Paul was called to the Chair of the Senate, *pro tempore;* and Isaac Blackford was elected Speaker of the House of Representatives.

On Thursday, November 7, the oath of office was administered to Governor Jennings and to Lieutenant-Governor Harrison, in the presence of both Houses; immediately after which, Gov. Jennings delivered his first message to the first General Assembly, under the first Constitution of the State of Indiana. In his message he said: " Gentlemen of the Senate and House of Representatives: The period has arrived which has devolved on you the important duty of giving the first impulse to the government of the State. The result of your deliberations will be considered as indicative of its future character, as well as of the future happiness and prosperity of its citizens. The reputation of the State, as well as its highest interest, will require that a just and generous policy toward the general Government, and a due regard to the rights of its members respectively, should invariably have their proper influence. In the commencement of the State government, shackles of the Colonial should be forgotten in your united exertions to prove, by happy experience, that a uniform adherence to the first principles of our Government, and a virtuous exercise of its powers, will best secure efficiency to its measures and stability to its character. Without a frequent recurrence to those principles, the administration of the government will imperceptibly become more and more arduous, until the simplicity of our republican institutions may eventually be lost in dangerous expedients and political design. Under every free government the happiness of the citizens must be identified with their morals; and while a constitutional exercise of their rights shall continue to have its due weight in the discharge of the duties required of the constituted authorities of the State, too much attention cannot be bestowed to the encouragement and promotion of every moral virtue, and to the enactment of laws calculated to restrain the vicious, and proscribe punishment for every crime commensurate to its enormity. In measuring, however, to each crime its adequate punishment, it will be well to recollect, that the certainty of punishment has generally the surest effect to prevent crime; while punishment unnecessarily severe, too often produces the acquittal of the guilty, and disappoints one of the greatest objects of legislation and good government.

The dessemination of useful knowledge will be indispensably necessary as a support to morals, and a restraint to vice; and on this subject, it will be necessary to direct your attention to the plan of education as prescribed by the Constitution. I recommend, to your consideration, the propriety of providing, by law, to prevent, more effectually, any unlawful attempts to seize, or carry into bondage persons of color legally entitled to their freedom; and at the same time, as far as practicable, to prevent those who rightfully owe service to the citizens of any other State or Territory, from seeking, within the limits of this State, a refuge from the possession of their lawful owners. Such a measure will tend to secure those who are free from any unlawful attempts to enslave them, and secure the rights of the citizens of the other States and Territories as far as ought reasonably to be expected."

The Territorial Government of Indiana, was thus superseded by a State Government, on the 7th of November, 1816; and the

State of Indiana was formally admitted into the Union by a joint resolution of Congress, approved on the 11th day of December, 1816.

———

Members of the second session of the General Assembly, of the State of Indiana, convened at Corydon, Monday, December 1st, 1817.

### SENATE.

From the counties of Knox, Sullivan, and Davies, William Polke.

From the counties of Warrick, Perry, and Posey, Daniel Grass.

From the county of Harrison, Dennis Pennington.

From the counties of Switzerland and Jefferson, John Paul.

From the county of Dearborn, Ezra Ferris.

From the county of Franklin, John Conner.

From the counties of Gibson and Pike, Isaac Montgomery.

From the counties of Washington, Orange, and Jackson, John DePauw.

From the county of Clark, James Beggs.

From the county of Wayne, Patrick Baird.

### HOUSE.

From the county of Posey, Samuel Conner and Dann Lynn.

From the county of Warrick, Ratcliff Boone.

From the county of Gibson, James Campbell and Richard Daniel.

From the county of Knox, Geo. R. C. Sullivan, John McClure and Robert Buntin.

From the county of Harrison, James B. Slaughter, Jacob Zenor, and William D. Littell.

From the county of Orange, Samuel Chambers.

From the county of Jackson, William Graham.

From the county of Washington, Samuel Milroy, and Alexander Littell.

From the county of Clark, Benjamin Ferguson, Thos. Carr, and Charles Beggs.

From the county of Jeffersoon, Williamsn Dunn and Nathaniel Hunt.

From the county of Switzerland, Ralph Cotton.

From the county of Dearborn, Amos Lane.

From the county of Franklin, Stephen C. Stephens, James Snowden, and John Bryson.

From the county of Wayne, Joseph Holman, John Scott, and Robert Hill.

Amos Lane, Speaker,
John F. Ross, Clerk, and
Robert Biggs, Doorkeeper.

Members of the third session of the General Assembly, convened at Corydon, Monday, December 7th, 1818.

### SENATE.

From the county of Wayne, Patrick Baird.

From the county of Franklin, John Conner.

From the county of Dearborn, Ezra Ferris.

From the counties of Jefferson and Switzerland, John Paul.

From the county of Clark, James Beggs.

From the counties of Washington, Jackson, Orange, Lawrence, and Monroe, John DePauw.

From the counties of Gibson, Pike, and Dubois, Isaac Montgomery.

From the counties of Harrison and Crawford, Dennis Pennington.

From the counties of Knox, Sullivan, Daviess, and Vigo, William Polke.

From the counties of Posey, Vanderburg, Perry. Spencer, and Warrick, Ratliff Boone.

### HOUSE.

From the county of Wayne, John Sutherland, Lewis Johnson, and Zachariah Ferguson.

From the county of Franklin, Jonathan McCarthy, Allen Christer, and James Gowdie.

From the county of Dearborn, John Watts and Erasmus Powell.

From the county of Switzerland, Ralph Cotton.

From the county of Jefferson, Nathaniel Hunt, and Williamson Dunn.

From the county of Clark, John H. Thompson, Charles Beggs, and Joseph Bartholomew.

From the county of Washington, Samuel Milroy and Jonathan Lyons.

From the county of Jackson, William Graham.

From the county of Orange, Samuel Chambers.

From the county of Harrison, William P. Thomasson, Harbin H. Moore, and Jas. B. Slaughter.

From the county of Perry, Samuel Conner.

From the county of Warrick, Elisha Harrison.

From the county of Gibson, Richard Daniel and Jno. Johnson.

From the county of Knox, Geo. R. C. Sullivan, Robert Buntin, and General W. Johnson.

At this session John Paul was elected President, *pro tempore*, of the Senate, John Dill, Secretary, and Henry Batman, Doorkeeper.

The House elected Williamson Dunn, Speaker, John F. Ross, Clerk, and Jno. Johnson, Doorkeeper.

Members from the fourth session of the General Assembly, convened at Corydon, December 6th, 1819.

SENATE.

From the counties of Wayne and Randolph, Patrick Baird.

From the counties of Clark and a part of Floyd, James Beggs.

From the counties of Harrison, Crawford, and a part of Floyd, Dennis Pennington.

From the counties of Gibson and Pike, Isaac Montgomery.

From the county of Dearborn, John Gray.

From the counties of Vanderburg, Posey, Warrick, Spencer, and Perry, Elisha Harrison.

From the counties of Switzerland, Jefferson, Jennings, and Ripley, William Cotton.

From the counties of Franklin and Fayette, William C. Drew.

From the counties of Washington, Orange, Jackson, Lawrence, and Monroe, Alexander Little.

## HOUSE.

From the county of Wayne, John Sutherland, Robert Hill, and Joseph Hollman.

From the county of Franklin, Allen Crisler, Enoch D. John, and Conrad Salor.

From the county of Dearborn, Isaac Morgan and Samuel Jelly.

From the county of Switzerland, Samuel Merrill.

From the county of Jefferson, Williamson Dunn and Jeremiah Sullivan.

From the county of Clark, John F. Ross, John H. Thompson, and Andrew P. Hay.

From the county of Jackson, William Graham.

From the county of Washington, Samuel Milroy and Samuel Lindley.

From the county of Orange, Samuel Chambers.

From the county of Harrison, William P. Thomasson, Jacob Zenor, and John N. Dunbar.

From the county of Perry, John Ewing.

From the county of Warrick, Daniel Grass.

From the county of Posey, Dann. Lynn.

From the counties of Knox, Sullivan, Vigo, Owen, and Daviess, Peter Allen.

From the county of Gibson, Robert M. Evans and John W. Maddox.

From the county of Knox, Thomas H. Blake and Joseph Warner.

At this session James Beggs was elected President, *pro tempore*, of the Senate, Henry Hurst, Secretary, and Henry Batman, Doorkeeper.

Williamson Dunn was elected Speaker of the House, William W. Mick, Clerk, and Andrew B. Holland, Doorkeeper.

Members of the fifth session of the General Assembly, convened at Corydon, November 27th, 1820.

SENATE.

From the counties of Knox, Sullivan, Vigo, Daviess, and Owen, William Polke.

From the counties of Franklin and a part of Fayette, William C. Drew.

From the counties of Warrick, Vanderburg, Posey, Spencer, Perry. and a part of Crawford, Elisha Harrison.

From the counties of Jefferson, Switzerland, Ripley, and Jennings, William Cotton.

From the counties of Harrison, Crawford, and Floyd, James B. Slaughter.

From the counties of Gibson, Posey, Dubois, and part of Perry, Richard Daniel.

From the counties of Washington, Orange, Jackson. Lawrence, and Monroe, James Gregory.

From the county of Clark and parts of Scott and Floyd, Joseph Bartholomew.

From the counties of Wayne, Randolph, and part of Fayette, Patrick Baird.

From the counties of Dearborn and Ripley, John Gray.

HOUSE.

From the county of Wayne, Joseph Hollman, Simon Yandes, and Thomas Swaine.

From the county of Franklin, James Goudie, Joseph Hanna, and Enoch D. John.

From the county of Dearborn, Ezra Ferris and Erasmus Powell.

From the county of Switzerland, Samuel Merrell.

From the county of Jefferson, Jeremiah Sullivan and Thomas Crawford.

From the county of Clark, John F. Ross, Andrew P. Hay, and Joseph Gibson.

From the county of Jackson, William Graham.

From the county of Washington, Maston G. Clark and Samuel Milroy.

From the county of Harrison, John Tipton, Henry Green, and Jacob Zenor.

From the county of Perry, Samuel Conner.

From the county of Warrick, Daniel Grass.

From the county of Franklin, Enoch D. John.

From the county of Posey, Chas. I. Battell.

From the county of Gibson, David Robb.

From the county of Knox, Geo. R. C. Sullivan, Rob't Sturgus, and John McDonald.

At this session James Morrison was elected Secretary of the Senate, and Henry Batman Doorkeeper.

William Graham was elected Speaker of the House, William W. Wick, Clerk, and Henry P. Thornton, Assistant Clerk, and John Moore, Doorkeeper.

----

Members of the sixth session, of the General Assembly, convened at Corydon, Monday, November 19, 1821.

### SENATE.

From the counties of Clark and Floyd, Joseph Bartholomew.

From the counties of Orange, Lawrence and Monroe, James Gregory.

From the counties of Gibson and Pike, Richard Daniel.

From the county of Dearborn, John Gray.

From the counties of Switzerland and Ripley, William Cotton.

From the counties of Knox, Daviess, and Martin, Frederick Sholtz.

From the counties of Sullivan, Vigo, Green, Owen, and Pike, Thomas H. Blake.

From the counties of Jefferson and Jennings, Brooke Bennett.

From the county of Washington, Marston G. Clark.

From counties of Harrison and Crawford, James B. Slaughter.

From the counties of Warrick, Vanderburg, and Posey, Elisha Harrison.

From the counties of Jackson and Bartholomew, William Graham.

From the county of Knox, General W. Johnson and Benj. S. Beckes.

From the counties of Daviess and Martin, James G. Reed.

From the county of Vigo, Joseph Shelby.

From the county of Jefferson, Copland P. J. Arion and Israel T. Canby.

From the county of Jennings, Zenas Kimberly.

From the county of Clark, John Miller and Jno. H. Thompson.

From the county of Floyd, Moses Kirkpatrick.

From the county of Washington, Samuel Milroy and Noah Wright.

From the county of Jackson, James Braman.

From the county of Scott, William D. Clark.

From the county of Orange, Chas. Dewey and Alexander Wallace.

From the county of Lawrence, John Milroy.

From the county of Monroe, David H. Maxwell.

From the county of Harrison, John Tipton and John N. Dunbar.

From the county of Crawford, Henry Green.

From the county of Posey, Charles I. Battell.

From the county of Gibson, William Prince.

From the counties of Vanderburg and Warrick, Hugh N. Donaghe.

From the counties of Spencer, Perry, and Dubois, Thomas Vandever.

From the county of Switzerland, Samuel Merrill and Wm. B. Chamberlain.

From the county of Ripley, Joseph Bentley.

From the county of Dearborn, Erasmus Powell, Amos Lane, and Ezra Ferris.

From the county of Bartholomew, John Lindsey.

From the county of Franklin, Geo. L. Murdock and James B. Ray.

From the county of Pike, John Johnson.

At this session James Morrison was elected Secretary of the Senate, Robt. A. New, Assistant Secretary, and Henry Batman Doorkeeper.

Samuel Milroy was elected Speaker of the House, John F. Ross, Clerk, Henry P. Thornton, Assistant Clerk, and John Moore, Doorkeeper.

Members of the seventh session of the General Assembly, convened at Corydon, Monday, December, 2, 1822.

### SENATE.

From the counties of Wayne and Randolph, Patrick Baird.
From the counties of Jefferson and Jennings, Brook Bennet.
From the counties of Gibson and Pike, Richard Daniel.
From the counties of Jackson, Scott, and Bartholomew, William Graham.
From the counties of Vanderburg, Warrick and Posey, Elisha Harrison.
From the counties of Harrison and Crawford, James B. Slaughter.
From the counties of Knox, Martin and Daviess, Frederick Scholtz.
From the counties of Clark and Floyd, John H. Thompson.
From the counties of Orange, Lawrence, and Monroe, Samuel Chambers.
From the counties of Sullivan, Vigo, Green, Owen, Parke, and Putnam, John Jenckes.
From the county of Dearborn, John Gray.
From the counties of Fayette and Union, Lewis Johnson.
From the counties of Spencer, Perry, Dubois, and Warrick, Daniel Grass.
From the county of Franklin, James B. Ray.
From the counties of Switzerland and Ripley, George Craig.

### HOUSE.

From the county of Knox, Benj. V. Beckes, and General W. Johnson.
From the counties of Daviess and Martin, William H. Rout.
From the county of Vigo, Lucius H. Scott.
From the county of Sullivan, Henry D. Palmer.
From the counties of Green, Owen, and Morgan, Hugh Barnes.

From the county of Jefferson, Milton Stapp and Nathaniel Hunt.

From the county of Jennings, William A. Bullock.

From the county of Clark, Isaac Howk and William W. Armstrong.

From the county of Floyd, Alexander S. Burnett.

From the county of Washington, Noah Wright.

From the county of Jackson, William Marshall.

From the county of Orange, John G. Clendenin and Jacob Molder.

From the county of Lawrence. Joseph Glover.

From the county of Monroe, Joshua H. Lucas.

From the county of Harrison, Dennis Pennington and Peter Mauck.

From the county of Crawford, Henry Green.

From the county of Posey, William Casey.

From the counties of Vanderburg and Warrick, Joseph Lane.

From the counties of Spencer, Perry and Dubois, John Daniel.

From the county of Randolph, John Wright.

From the county of Wayne, Robt. Hill, Isaac Julian, and John Jordan.

From the county of Fayette, Oliver H. Smith.

From the county of Union, Sylvester Everts.

From the county of Franklin, William McClary and Jno. E. Bush.

From the county of Switzerland, John Dumont and Lewis Scoville.

From the county of Dearborn, Pinkney James, Horace Bassett, and Ezekiel Jackson.

From the county of Ripley, Joseph Bentley.

From the county of Scott, Wm. Clark.

At this session William Graham was elected President, *pro tempore*, of the Senate, James Dill, Secretary, John H. Farnham, Assistant Secretary, and Isaac Ash, Doorkeeper.

General W. Johnson was elected Speaker of the House, Jno. F. Ross, Clerk, Henry P. Thompson, Assistant Clerk, and Jno. Moore, Doorkeeper.

Members of the eighth session of the General Assembly, convened at Corydon, Monday, December 1st, 1823.

From the counties of Warrick, Vanderburg, and Posey, Elisha Harrison.

From the counties of Spencer, Perry, and Dubois, Daniel Grass.

From the counties of Martin, Knox, and Daviess, Frederick Sholtz.

From the counties of Jackson, Scott, and Bartholomew, William Graham.

From the counties of Switzerland and Ripley, George Craig.

From the county of Dearborn, John Gray.

From the county of Franklin, James B. Ray.

From the counties of Fayette and Union, Lewis Johnson.

From the counties of Gibson and Pike, Isaac Montgomery.

From the counties of Orange, Monroe, and Lawrence, Samuel Chambers.

From the county of Washington, Samuel Milroy.

From the counties of Clark and Floyd, John H. Thompson.

From the counties of Jefferson and Jennings, Milton Stapp.

From the counties of Wayne and Randolph, James Raridon.

From the counties of Marion, Hamilton, Madison, Johnson, Decatur, Shelby, Rush and Henry, James Gregory.

From the counties of Harrison and Crawford, James B. Slaughter.

HOUSE.

From the county of Knox, John Law and James B. McCall.

From the counties of Daviess and Martin, James G. Reed.

From the counties of Vigo and Parke, Thomas H. Black.

From the county of Sullivan, Henry D. Palmer.

From the counties of Greene, Owen and Morgan, Eli Dixon.

From the county of Jefferson, David Hillis and C. P. J. Arion.

From the county of Jennings, William A. Bullock.

From the county of Clark, Rouben W. Nelson and Wm. G. Armstrong.

From the county of Floyd, Alexander S. Burnett.

From the county of Washington, Ezra Childs and Alex. Huston.

From the county of Jackson, William Marshall.

From the county of Scott, William D. Clark.

From the county of Orange, John G. Clendenin and Ezekiel S. Riley.

From the county of Lawrence, Vincent Williams.

From the county of Monroe, David H. Maxwell.

From the county of Crawford, Elisha Tadlock.

From the county of Harrison, Dennis Pennington and John Zenor.

From the county of Posey, John Schnell.

From the county of Gibson, John Milbourn.

From the county of Pike, John Johnson.

From the counties of Vanderburg and Warrick, Robert M. Evans.

From the counties of Spencer, Perry and Dubois, David Edwards.

From the county of Randolph, John Wright.

From the county of Wayne, Robert Hill and Abel Lomax.

From the county of Union, Sylvanus Everts.

From the county of Franklin, Geo. L. Murdock and David Oliver.

From the county of Switzerland, Stephen C. Stephens and Ralph Cotton.

From the county of Ripley, Robert Kennedy.

From the county of Dearborn, Samuel Jelly, Benjamin J. Blythe and David Bowers.

From the county of Bartholomew, Benjamin Irwin.

From the county of Fayette, James Browulee.

From the counties of Marion, Madison, Hamilton and Johnson, James Paxton.

From the counties of Henry, Rush, Decatur, and Shelby, Thomas Hendricks.

From the counties of Putnam, Montgomery, and Wabash, Amos Robertson.

David H. Maxwell, Speaker.

Henry P. Thornton, Principal Clerk.

James E. D. Lanier, Assistant Clerk.

James M. Ray, Enrolling Clerk.

John Moore, Doorkeeper.

The Senate, at this session, elected Jas. Dill, Secretary, John H. Farnham, Assistant Secretary, John Medcap, Doorkeeper.

OLD CAPITAL HOTEL.

The principal Hotel building at which the members of the Constitutional Convention of 1816, and the members of the General Assemblies that followed, while Corydon was the State Capital. boarded, was built in 1809, by Jacob Conrad, a gentleman who came from Pennsylvania.

It is located about one mile east of the Capital building. When we consider the many privations of the people of those times, that they traveled many miles, over a roadless country, to reach the State Capital, it is no surprise that they would go one mile to secure good lodging. This ancient hotel is constructed of hard blue limestone, taken from an inexhaustible quarry of the immediate vicinity.

The above is an exact front view of the old building taken from a photograph obtained in August last. There are many rooms in this building. The walls are twenty feet high, and eighteen inches thick. The end and side, as seen in the view, are about twenty feet long, each. That the reader in this progressive age of architecture may comprehend something of the magnitude of this old hotel, setting out in the country, on the pike. leading from Corydon to New Albany, we will state that the weight of masonry in it. as estimated by a civil engineer, is 618,790 tons. The superficial feet of flooring 3,412, which is of blue ash. The joice were prepared with the broad-axe and whip-saw. All the wood work, not exposed, remains in a perfect state of preservation. The giant walls remain intact. And mortar used seems impervious, though having been exposed to the elements more than eighty years. The material for this mortar was procured not more than one hundred yards from the old building. As to the durability of the work done on this building, and of the material it contains, the structure itself gives evidence that centuries may come and go but the hotel of the fathers will still stand.

The small stone building near by, is a spring-house through which flows a magnificent spring of excellent lime stone water. It is said that some of the guests were very fond of taking a a portion of this water with their "malarial medicine," which was a preventative to "chills and ague" in those days.

The old hotel is now owned by Joseph J. Terstegge, a worthy and progressive citizen of New Albany, Ind.

### MISCELLANEOUS.

On Monday, the 3rd day of March, 1817, the citizens of Corydon met to consider the propriety of incorporating the town. Gen. John Tipton was called to preside over their deliberations, and Reuben W. Nelson was elected Secretary of the meeting. The opinion of the qualified voters was taken and the following expressed themselves favorable to incorporation:

| | |
|---|---|
| Joseph McMahon, | Anthony Gwartney, |
| David S. Collins, | James Kirkpatrick, |
| George Jones, | Patrick Flanagan, |
| Wm. P. Thomasson, | Jonathan Houser, |
| H. P. Coburn, | John T. Jameson, |
| Milo R. Davis, | William Johnson, |
| Daniel Craig, | A. Brandon, |
| Dudley Gresham, | Henry Rice, Jr., |
| Lyman Beeman, | Thomas Spencer, |
| Robert A. New, | William Smith, |
| Harbin H. Moore, | Ezekiel Wood, |
| James G. Smith, | Samuel Ruth, |
| James B. Slaughter. | |

There being no opposition to incorporating, it was so ordered.

On Monday, the 17th day March, 1817, the qualified voters met at the Court House, in Corydon, for the purpose of electing five Trustees for said town. Gen. John Tipton presided, and Davis Floyd was chosen Clerk of the election; when the following persons were elected by ballot to serve one year: Henry Rice, Richard M. Heth, A. D. Thom, James Kirkpatrick and Mil R. Davis.

---

### HARRISON COUNTY'S FIRST OFFICERS.

Patrick Shields, Presiding Judge.
John G. Pfrimmer and Moses Boone, Associate Judges.
Geo. F. Pope. Clerk and Recorder, and
Spier Spencer, Sheriff and Treasurer.

### PRESENT OFFICERS.

Charles W. Cole, Auditor.
Patrick Griffin, Treasurer.
Alvin E. Smith, Clerk.
Clabe H. Shuck, Sheriff.
Lewis M. O'Bannon, Recorder.
Andrew J. Armstrong, Surveyor.
Michael Gleitz, Coroner.
Harrison Pitman, Anthony Kannapel and William Richert, Commissioners.
Daniel J. Bowling will succeed Pitman in December, next.
Charles W. Thomas, County Superintendent of Schools.
Silas Bringle, County Assessor.

---

The following served as State Officers while the State Capital was at Corydon:

### GOVERNORS.

Jonathan Jennings, from Nov. 7, 1816, to December 4th, 1822.
William Hendricks, from Dec. 4, 1822, to Feb. 12, 1825.

## LIEUTENANT GOVERNORS.

Christopher Harrison, from 1816 to 1819.
Ratliff Boone, from 1819 to 1825.

## SECRETARY OF STATE.

Robert A. New. from 1816 to 1825.

## AUDITOR OF STATE.

William H. Lilly, from 1816 to 1829.

## TREASURERS OF STATE.

Daniel C. Lane, from 1816 to 1823.
Samuel Merrill, from 1823 to 1835.

## JUDGES OF THE SUPREME COURT.

James Scott. from 1816 to 1831.
John Johnson, from 1816 to 1817.
Jesse L. Holman, from 1816 to 1831.
Isaac Blackford, from 1817 to 1853.

## UNITED STATES SENATORS.

James Noble, from 1816 to 1831.
Waller Taylor. from 1816 to 1825.

## REPRESENTATIVES IN CONGRESS.

William Hendricks. from 1817 to 1822.
William Prince, from 1822 to 1824, (died.)
Jacob Call, from 1824, (to fill vacancy.)

GOVERNOR'S MANSION.

The above is a complete illustration of the front view of the Governor's Mansion, which was photographed in the summer of 1891. It is located about two squares north-east of the old Capitol building, on a romantic elevation. overlooking the major portion of the ancient town of Corydon.

It is about thirty-two feet long, two stories high, each twelve feet in the clear, two rooms in each story, and double-story L attached to the east-half of the rear. about sixteen feet long.

Here resided Governors Thomas Posey. Jonathan Jennings and William Hendricks.

It is a brick structure. and while it is in a fair state of preservation. it is plain to be seen that time. the great destroyer, has lain his hands upon it; too much dilapidated to be used as a residence. It is the property of Dr. Alma E. L. Smith, one of our oldest and most respected citizens.

The following antique records are found in the county offices at Corydon. On Commissioner's Record August 13th, 1817, the following:

"On application of Ebenezer McDonald, Esqr., Clerk of the Supreme Court of the State of Indiana, by Davis Floyd, it is ordered that Mr. McDonald be permitted to keep his office in the north-east corner room of the upper story of the Court house when the said room is not occupied by any court of Indiana, or the Legislature."

"Ordered that John Tipton be allowed the sum of four dollars and fifty cents, with interest, for so much money advanced for wolf scalps, killed previous to the late law, as per certificate filed, and that the county Treasurer pay the same out of this years levy."

"Ordered that the Sheriff do on this day let out to the lowest bidder the cleaning of lot No. 44, being one acre & — perches and the cleaning half of the streets adjoining the same, and also the building of a stray pen, of hewed logs, twenty-four feet square, to be fixed on nine good blocks two feet long, one of the feet sunk in the ground—the pen to be six feet high including the one foot of the blocks—to have girders across the corners well pinned on, the door to be faced and well pinned on and a strong shutter to the door with a common padlock, and that the said Sheriff take bond with good security in double the amount of the lowest bid, to be completed within four months. The money to be paid at the expiration of the time aforesaid."

(Tuesday April 4, 1809.)

"Ordered that the Sheriff of Harrison county collect agreeably to law and agreeably to the Commissioners list from each person chargable therewith on each horse, mare, &c., above three years old, fifty cents, and on each slave one dollar, on each — horse the rates of the season, on each Ferry, except George Doups, four dollars, on Geo. Doups ferry two dollars, on each tavern licensed four dollars, on each one hundred dollars valuation of land ten cents, and pay to the county claimants the sums respectively allowed.

Ordered that the taverns be rated as follows, to-wit:

For each quart of whisky............................... 37½ cts.
For every quart of bounce .......................... 37½ "
"    "    "    " brandy (French)................ $1.50

| | | | | | |
|---|---|---|---|---|---|
| For every quart of peach brandy | | | | 37½ cts. | |
| " | " | pint | " whisky | 18¾ | " |
| " | " | " | " bounce | 25 | " |
| " | " | " | " French brandy | 75 | " |
| " | " | " | " peach brandy | 18¾ | " |
| " | " | half pint of whisky | | 12½ | " |
| " | " | " | " bounce | 18¾ | " |
| " | " | " | " French brandy | 50 | " |
| " | " | " | " peach brandy | 12½ | " |
| for a breakfast & dinner each | | | | 25 | " |
| for supper | | | | 25 | " |
| for a cold breakfast, dinner & supper each | | | | 16½ | " |
| for a horse per night stabling and hay | | | | 25 | " |
| for a feed of grain per gallon | | | | 12½ | " |
| lodging per night | | | | 12¼ | " " |

(Wednesday, April, 5, 1809.)

### "JOHN ELLIOT TO JOHN GEORGE PFRIMMER.

"Know all men by these presents that I John Elliot of the county of Knox, and Indiana Territory, have for and in consideration of the sum of four hundred dollars, to me in hand paid at or before the inseating & delivery hereof bargained, and do by these presents bargain and sell, unto John George Pfrimmer, of the county of Harrison, in said Territory, a certain negro woman named Betty, with her mulatto child, named Selina, which said negro & child was purchased of my father Robert Elliot, of the said county of Knox, by bill of sale dated on the 7th of January last past which said bill of sale with its conditions & assurances I do hereby assign and guarantee unto the said Pfrimmer, his heirs and assigns, and will by these presents warrant and defend.

Given under my hand and seal in the said county of Harrison, this 10th day of Feb., 1811.    John Elliott.    (Seal.)
In presence of the words
"four hundred & woman"
being first indented.
William Henry Harrison,
Henry Rice.
Recorder's office 15th March, 1811.    I Richard M. Heth,

recorder of Harrison county, do certify that I have recorded the within Bill of Sale in my office.

R. M. HETH, Recorder."

BOONE TO CURRANCE.

"This indenture made the 11th day of October in the year of our Lord, one thousand eight hundred and eleven between Squire Boone of Harrison county, Indiana Territory of the one part, and Thomas Currance of the State of Kentucky and county of Henry of the other part witnesseth that the said Squire Boone for and in consideration of the sum of fifty pounds current money to him the said Boone in hand paid the receipt whereof he doth hereby confess & acknowledge, hath given, granted, bargained, sold and confirmed, unto the said Thomas Currance, his heirs & assigns one tract or parcel of land lying and being in Henry county out of a 2000 acre survey made in the name of said Boone seventy-five acres, Beginning at a hickory, Ash, and white Oak, thence N. 45 E. west the old line 72 poles to a white oak and two black oaks, Thence S. 45 E. 167 to a white oak, dog wood & hickory, Thence S. 45 W 72 poles to a hickory, beach and red oak, Thence N. 45 W. 167 poles to the beginning. To have and to hold the said 75 acres of land be the same more or less with all and singular the appurtenances thereunto belonging unto the said Thomas Currance his heirs or assigns to the only proper use and benefit & behoof of him the said Currance forever, and him the said Boone for himself his heirs assigns the said 75 acres of land with all the appurtenances unto the said Thomas Currance his heirs or assigns against the claim or claims of any person or persons claiming by from or under him the said Boone will warrant & forever defend.

In witness whereof I have hereunto set my hand and affixed my seal the day and year first above written

SQUIRE BOONE        (Seal.)

Recorders Office October 11, 1811.

I, Richard M. Heth, recorder of Harrison County, Indiana Territory, do certify that I have recorded the within deed in my office this 11th day of October 1811.

R. M. HETH."

41

"The President laid before the Senate a written communication from R. A. New, Esquire, Secretary of State, relative to sundry contracts for printing the laws &c. &c. as follows to-wit: To the Honorable the President of the Senate of the State of Indiana:

In obedience to an existing law of this State, the Secretary thereof respectively represents, that the following contracts have been entered into for and on the part of the State.

A. & J. Brandon have contracted to print the bills, laws and journals of the General Assembly for 50 cents per thousand Ms, and 50 cents per token press work; with the addition of 50 per cent. for figured, and one hundred per cent. for ruled and figured work—the paper being a separate charge at cost and carriage. The work to be done in a workmanlike manner, on good type, at the rate of thirty-two octave pages per week, if required; and they will fold and stitch the same, and have them ready for delivery in a week after the printing is done, at the following rates: If the book contains not more than twenty signatures, at six dollars per hundred, if more, at 10 dollars per hundred copies. But nothing in this contract is to be so construed as to prevent an application to the Legislature for a further compensation, if the money be not paid within thirty days after the work is completed. They contracted also to furnish the Legislature with stationery at the following rates: letter or post paper at 5 dollars per ream; writing or cap, No 1, at 5 dollars, No 2, at 4 dollars 50 cents, and No, 3 at 4 dollars; quills, wafers and ink-powder at the current retailing prices—subject to the same provisions as to payment. Ephraim Gwartney has contracted to furnish the Legislature with fuel at ninety-eight cents per day.

Bond and approved security has been given for the faithful discharge of their several contracts.

I have the honor to be sir, very respectfully,
Your obedient Servant,
R. A. NEW,
Secretary of State."
(*From Senate Journal, December 9,* 1818.)

THE HARRISON PLACE.

Gen. William Henry Harrison, Governor of Indiana Territory, from 1800 to 1812, the ninth President of the United States, and Grandfather of the present President of the United States, Benjamin Harrison, of Indiana, bought of the General Government, in an early day, all of section 19, township 3, south of range 3 east; also a part of section 30, township 3, south of range 3 east. This land is all in one body and contains 829.20 acres, It is situated about six miles north-west of Corydon, and four miles north-east of the famous Wyandotte cave on the Blue river. Here, in 1801, the Governor erected a house and planted an orchard. The varieties of apples of his selection were Green Pippin and Romanite. On the first day of this month, October, we visited this sacred spot, in company with an artist, and photographed three of the apple trees still standing, and the above is an exact view of the same. As will be seen in the view one is dead; one partially so, but the other is still vigorous and full of fruit. The apples we gathered from it on that day weighed one pound each; they being of the Romanite variety. The trees photographed are quite lofty, and three feet in diameter, two feet from their base. The General's old residence is gone. Only the excavation of the old cellar, the stones that held its walls intact, and a few logs that tumbled from the walls of this ancient residence into this excavation, together with a few small trees and shrubs remain to mark the spot, which may be seen just to the rear of these giant and ancient apple trees. The "Governor's field" is located a short distance south of the old orchard. The "General's meadow" about the same distance north of the orchard. One-fourth mile north-east of the orchard is the noted "Harrison Spring," eighty feet in diameter, and though it has been sounded over four hundred feet, no bottom has been reached. It rises from a solid rock in a level spot of land, and it has a sufficient flow of water to turn a valuable flour mill, and a saw mill, throughout the year, on the banks of the Blue river, into which stream it flows, where General Harrison built his mill in 1805. One hundred yards west of this gigantic spring was erected a distillery in early times; and one of the attractive features to the Indians and early white settlers hereabout was the process of pumping water from the spring to the distillery by a dog.

The "Harrison place" was one of the principal recruiting points for Capt. Spier Spencer's company, that fought so bravely under the old "Hero of Tippecanoe," on the 7th of November, 1811. Capt. Spencer and two of his lieutenants, McMahon and Berry, fell in this engagement. While governor of Indiana territory, and even afterward, Gen. Harrison spent much of his time on his farm and about Corydon, and no

44

one ever rendered greater or more valuable services to the people of Indiana, and especially to those of Harrison county, than did General William Henry Harrison, who was in the public service of his country, from his youth until his death; and the fact that the present President is his grandson, only perpetuates his illustrious name. The records in the Recorder's office of Harrison county, show that William Henry Harrison and his wife Anna, on the 6th day of July, 1817, deeded the land mentioned to Joshua Wilson and Abijah Bayless for the consideration of ten thousand dollars.

HONORABLE MENTION.

Col. Thomas Posey, Territorial Governor, from 1813 to 1816, resided at Corydon many years, and his home was here when he died in 1860.

Gen. John Tipton, resided at Corydon, and served in the office of Sheriff of the county, was Representative in the Legislature several terms, and elected United States Senator, from Indiana, and served from 1831 to 1839. He died at his home in Logansport, Cass county, in 1839. He was an able man, and one of the most conspicuous personages in the State, during his time.

Davis Floyd, lived at Corydon for several years, was a Judge of the Common Pleas Court, and was considered an able jurist.

Dennis Pennington, was one of the first settlers of Harrison county, served in both branches of the Legislature about twenty years; and was elected Speaker of the Territorial House of Representatives.

Harbin H. Moore, was a brilliant attorney, who made his home at Corydon, in early times, frequently represented Harrison County in the State Legislature, and was elected Speaker of the House in the eleventh, twelfth and sixteenth sessions.

William A. Porter, resided at Corydon, until his death, about eight years ago. He was an able attorney, was Judge of the Common Pleas Court, served in both branches of the Legislature, at various times, and was elected speaker of the House in the thirty-second session.

Nathaniel Albertson, resided in Morgan township, this

county, and represented this Congressional district in Congress in the 31st session.

SQUIRE BOONE, brother of Daniel Boone, the celebrated pioneer, lived and died in Harrison county. His remains are interred in a cave in the southern part of the county near where he died.

JOSIAH LINCOLN, uncle of President Abraham Lincoln, lived and died in Blue River township, Harrison county, where he has many descendants now living.

SIMEON K. WOLFE, was an honored and highly respected citizen of Corydon, where he spent most of his life in the practice of law. He represented this district in Congress during the 43d session.

ALLEN D. THOM, of Corydon, was a noted man in early days. He was Adjutant General of the State, and for many years private secretary to the Governors.

GEN. JAMES C. VEACH, a gallant commander in the late war, was born and reared in Taylor township, Harrison county.

JUDGE WALTER Q. GRESHAM, of the 7th Judicial Circuit of the United States, the upright and able jurist, soldier and statesman, was born and reared in Harrison county. He read and practiced law in Corydon, from whence he was elected a member of the Legislature in 1860. When the tocsin of war sounded in 1861, he responded to the call of his country, and was made Colonel of the 53d Ind. Vol. Infantry. He was rapidly promoted for gallantry. Few men, indeed, in the employment of the United States, acquired so deserving a fame as Judge Gresham. He rose from obscurity to eminence. Reputation fell not on him as the dews or as the snows fall; he toiled for it, bled for it. He has been the builder of the edifice of his name, has gained a splendid renown, and ascended the acclivitous path of military and judicial glory to honorable heigths of enviable fame.

CAPT. SPIER SPENCER, was one of the early settlers of Corydon. He was the first Sheriff of Harrison county. He commanded a company of soldiers, under General William Henry Harrison, at the battle of Tippecanoe, and fell early in the action. He was a good citizen, a brave and gallant soldier. Descendants of his, still live in Corydon, good and useful citizens.

HON. JOHN MATHES, one of the members of the constitutional convention of 1850, from this county, is still living at the advanced age of eighty-one years. " Uncle " John came to this county with his parents from Kentucky, while this state was a territory, where he has lived ever since. He has lived an honorable and upright life, highly respected by all who know him. He has served as State Senator, and filled many other stations of public trust, to which his constituents called him, with ability and fidelity to the public interests that meet the approbation of all. Although more than eighty years of age, he is yet as spry and active as most men at half his age. Long may he live to enjoy the benefits and blessings of the government he assisted in forming.

HON. S. M. STOCKSLAGER, member of Congress from this district, from 1880 to 1884, and United States Land Commissioner under President Cleveland, was born and reared in this county, and since his majority, has made his home in Corydon. He was elected to the State Senate in 1874. In every position he gained the respect and confidence of his constituents. He was a gallant soldier in the late war, serving in two different regiments, the 38 Ind. Infantry, and the 13th Indiana Cavalry. He enlisted as a private and came out a Captain. He is a man of ability and energy, commended by all who know him, for his lofty spirit of honor, spotless integrity, kindness of heart, and promptness of decision.

COL. WILLIAM W. KINTNER, of the Kintner hotel, Corydon, is the oldest native born male inhabitant of Corydon. The gallant and jolly Colonel is a kind and generous hearted gentleman. He is known, perhaps, more extensively than any other private citizen in Indiana. He is courteous and kind, a worthy, influential and valuable citizen.

MAJ. WILLIAM T. JONES, of the 17th Ind. Infantry (Wilders), and later Associate Justice of, and Delegate in Congress from Wyoming territory, was a native of Corydon, and spent most of his life here. Perhaps one of the brainiest and most brilliant men this part of the state ever produced was Major Jones. He entered the army while yet a boy, as lieutenant of his company, and for gallantry and merritorious service rose rapidly to Major of his regiment. He was a man of great honor and strict integrity; and he justly merited the bold prominence of being associated in that galaxy of young, brilliant and dashing officers of the late war, whose valor and genious were developed on its many and sanguinary fields. His death a few years ago was lamented by all who knew him.

Hon. WILLIAM T. ZENOR, is the learned, pure, able and upright Judge, of the 3d Judicial Circuit of Indiana, who presides in the "Ancient Capitol" building. His grand father, Jacob Zenor, was a member from Harrison county, of the first general assembly of the State of Indiana. Judge Zenor's father, Col. Philip Zenor, was a gallant officer in the Mexican war. The brave and gallant old hero is still living honored by all who know him.

PROF. JAMES G. MAY, a pioneer teacher, resided at Corydon many years and was regarded as an excellent instructor.

PROF. JOSEPH P. FUNK, of the New Albany schools, is a native of Harrison county. He resided at the old Capital town for quite a period, instructing the many pupils placed under his care. No one ever rendered more valuable services, or attained greater popularity, as an instructor, than did Prof. Funk, at Corydon. He was regarded as an excellent scholar and an able and conscientious instructor.

Hon. THOMAS C. SLAUGHTER, Judge of the 3d Judicial Circuit, who died in that honorable position in 1878, was one of Corydon's most respected and honored citizens. The citizens honored him with many positions of trust. His father, Dr. James B. Slaughter, was also a worthy citizen of Corydon, who served with ability in both branches of the Legislature, while Corydon was the State Capital, and also at Indianapolis.

Hon. DANIEL C. LANE, the first Treasurer of State, was a citizen of Corydon, and was honored with many positions of public trust.

Hon. C. W. COOK, is the very efficient Prosecuting Attorney, who looks after the pleas of the State, in the Ancient Capitol building. Mr. Cook is a good citizen of Corydon, an able lawyer, an eloquent and forcible speaker, with a bright future.

COL. GEO. W. FRIEDLY, late of Chicago, was a native of this county. He was a brave and gallant soldier, and an able attorney.

Space forbids that more of the many good and great men who have lived in and about Corydon, or have had business transactions here, be mentioned.